poe

FOR MEN

who

DREAM

of

LOLITA

KIM MORRISSEY

COTEAU BOOKS

Also by Kim Morrissey:
Batoche (Coteau Books, 1989; reprinted 1990 and 1992)
Studio One: Stories for Radio (contributor, Coteau Books, 1990)
Dora (available in Playwrights Union of Canada Library)

Edited by Don Kerr.
Cover photograph by Nicolas Gyenes of a replica of the left panel of the Ludovisi Throne, circa 460 B.C.—"Hetaera" or "Flute Player." The original is located in the Musee de Thermes in Rome. Photograph courtesy of the University of Saskatchewan, Museum of Antiquities.
Book design by Shelley Sopher, Coteau Books.
Typeset by Val Jakubowski, Coteau Books.
Printed and bound in Canada.

Quotations from *Lolita* by Vladimir Nabokov are reproduced with the permission of the publisher, Weidenfeld and Nicolson Ltd. in the U.K. and Commonwealth countries, and Smith/Skolnik in the U.S. The epigraph on page vii is found on page 11 of *Lolita*, Weidenfeld and Nicolson Ltd., eighth impression, January 1984; the "prologue" on page 71 is found on pages 5 and 6.

The publisher gratefully acknowledges the financial assistance of the Saskatchewan Arts Board, the Canada Council and the Department of Communications.

The author would like to thank the Canada Council for the short term grant to complete the first draft of this manuscript, and Brenda Niskala, Katerina Anghelaki-Rooke, Patrick Lane and her late husband, Roy Morrissey, for their advice and encouragement.

Some of these poems have appeared previously in *Prism, Contemporary Verse Two, Grain, (m)other tongues, NeWest Review, Other Voices, People to People, Bête Noire,* and *Poetry Canada Review,* and the anthologies *Kitchen Talk* (Red Deer College Press, forth-coming) and *More Garden Varieties Two* (League of Canadian Poets, AYA Press).

Canadian Cataloguing in Publication Data

Morrissey, Kim, 1955-

Poems for men who dream of Lolita

Poems.
ISBN 1-55050-030-9 (bound) - 1-55050-029-5 (pbk.)

I. Title.

PS8576.074I7F6   1992   C811'.54   C92-098016-3
PR9199.3.M67F6 1992

COTEAU BOOKS
401 - 2206 Dewdney Ave.
Regina, SK Canada
S4R 1H3

To Jim Garrard
for *Cold Comfort*

She was Lo, plain Lo, in the morning,
standing four foot ten in one sock.
She was Lola in slacks.
She was Dolly at school.
She was Dolores on the dotted line.
But in my arms
she was always Lolita.

Nabokov, *Lolita*

part one: 1947

I am the Book of Dolores B. Haze
otherwise known as Dolly
(sometimes as Lo) age twelve
and almost a quarter

I come with a curse

and my pages
are private

if you read me, be warned

I am the Book of Dolores
beware:

put me back in my box
and be happy

Saturday, April 23

Kenny Knight
throwing papers at dusk
from his bike at the curb
has skin like a dipper of water
and quarters warm to the touch

and to talk! to talk and
to watch Kenny's eyes
glance up and then down
dark and then gone
leaving only the scent of Ivory
the end of a smile

and the thin crease
of a remembered scar
trailing down his left cheek
like a dream

Secrets: 1

Our new Lodger has been known
to use *Man's Prerogative*
to pee off our porch
in the dark

Mummy doesn't approve

but Hummy
just buttons his buttons
and says: finished.
no longer a topic
a man is a man
is a man
but Mummy says no

pee kills plants

Secrets: 2

there's a man that I know
that's a writer that
likes me so much
I could live at his house
and be famous

but mummy said no

he sends letters and plays
and green leather-book poems
silk stockings with pink satin seams
a glass slipper charm

mummy doesn't approve

but when I'm sixteen
and can do what I like
I'm going, I'll go, I'll be gone

don't tell mother

Secrets: 3

last year the man who is famous
the man I adore
said he liked to see
little girls curls
brushed my cheek

everyone laughed

but sometimes I wake dreaming
his cigarette in my mouth
the warm weight of his arm

one hand dreaming
the dark stones in his ring

round as the pearls
Mama wears for our Lodger
dark as my father's dead eyes

Saturday Matinee, June 3

today Kenny Knight
put his hand on my knee
I said no and stared at the screen

tasting the butter-salt corn
the clean warmth of boy skin
the hot breath

I said no, meaning do
what you like, Kenny Knight

but don't ask

don't tell mother I've
nibbled your sausage
don't tell mummy I've
scoffed all your bread
and whatever you do
don't tell the old witch
I've stained her best
spoon in the egg!

Tuesday, June 6

Mr. Humbert Humbert
Mr. Humbert Squared
likth to do everything twithe
twithe
which drives my mudder mad
mad

he has two cups of coffee
and two slices of toast
he brushes and shaves
and flushes
twice just to be sure

once,
when I had an eyelash
he closed mummy's door
and licked my bare eye
like a snail

and then licked the other
and then two times more

and then Mr. Hum
Bert Humbert Squared
blinked twice and said
not to tell Mother

tell her what?

Saturday, June 10

when is a door not a door
I ask hummy
coming into his room
—when it's a jar
when it's a what?
a jar
you know, ajar.
and what's that?
it means open

oh

this too is open
this desk
this drawer
come see
come

come
sit on my lap

and look:
a trick!
when I spread your knees wide
with my legs you are caught

why did the fly fly?
because the spider
spied her

Last night in the hammock
he called me "Lolita"
playing hand over hand over hand

No. My name is Dolores, age twelve
grade six, size three
my friends call me Dolly

Lie still little apple pie sweet
your name from now on is Lolita
leg over leg over leg
and you need your cheeks pinched
like a pie crust   pressed down
two fingers two fingers two

Just a prick and she's done
says my mother and purses her lips
peering into her mirror
as she put on her eyes
Dumpy Dolly

My name is Dolores

My friends call me Dolly, but
my name's really Dolores

My name is Dolores, age twelve

August 16, 1947

here is where we start
here between the long ride home
from a camp full of sand and canoes
and a mother who does not send love
you ask for two beds
and one room

here is the place we remain
playing with ice cubes, toying with spoons
charging the cheque to our room

here is where you tell me to bathe
folding my clothes on your pillow
towelling my hair

here is the red quilt from my bed
thrown down on the floor
feet sticky with heat from the bath
pink toes cupping the tiles

here is the quilt on the bed that we share
and here,
here is where we start counting

stepfather

somewhere between the dark stain
on the tiles
and the towels
heaped on the back of the toilet
you rest your case:
I may leave if I want
today you are giving me choices

I watch my head turn in the mirror
thin hair finger-brushed back
tied low on my neck like a bone
taste your hair at the back of my throat
tightly wound wires
riding the tip of my tongue

today is the day we make choices:
you or the foster home
you or the jail

14

I am holding my tongue like a fist
pressed hard against teeth
the smell of stale blood in my throat
as you breathe through my mouth

when I close my eyes I hear summer
the clatter of bicycles, green bottled cokes
the kissing and telling and arms folded tight
the thin whisper of secrets not told

it is summer and we are alone
with only the weight of moist air
pushing sweat through my lungs
and the faint pulse of insects
singing blood

and now it's the mouth
the mouth and the tongue
pressed down
to the faint smell of sea

think of lollipops
not mouldy socks
close your eyes
tight, think sour cream

don't think cheese, don't
see raw sausage left too long
in the heat

think ice cream

you scream, we all
hold my tongue
swallow hard

and relax

16

sometimes I dream he's my mother

I'm a starlet, a floozie
a whore in this movie
or he's dying, and my body's a gift

              I'm a beautiful princess

he's a prince
all he needs is a kiss

sometimes
I pretend my dead mother
stands at the foot of the bed
saying *practice*

              makes perfect

sometimes I wake
dreaming blood

17

last night I dreamed the old schoolyard
the pony sweet smell of cut grass
bare knees warm from the sun

> motel carpets
> the colour of money
> sausage fingers that pry
> like rough worms

and Kenny shaking prisms for hair
spins the ball and floats it suspended
just kissing the plate

> on the bedsheets
> a faint flowering of blood
> like dried weeds
> pressed to wax paper

and on the walk home we share secrets
blood bricks warming our backs
one leg holding the wall

> in a room full of old
> air and stale cat piss
> ammonia and Floral
> Delight

the slow sudden kiss
the sweat of his lips after softball
tastes like mine

18

I wake to the wet slap of sweat
moving skin against skin
the dry rattle of lungs

eyes open, I hear your hand fisted
rubbing hard to the beat of the clock
the creak of the bed in the dark

the sheet that we share
burns like stubble

you are going blind, growing hairs
damned to hell, and I am here
far away from your hands and your eyes
dreaming ice

dreaming Alaska

evening again and I stand
as he kneels at my feet
rubbing skin from my skin
as he lectures and scrubs:

particular attention must be paid
to the cracks: between toes
behind knees under nails
particular attention
the sly glance to the side

I stand still in his bath
feeling goose-bumps
forming under stale steam

knowing
cracks too small for the sponge
will be licked

these nights fold into themselves
like a deck of old cards
no one bothers to shuffle
no one wins

these are the moments before waiting
the cracks between words   the years
I say nothing and pretend
I am only a child

this is the princess in the tower
letting down her slick hair
keeping one strand beautifully
braided in secret for the man

who wants only
to take her away

when I remember
I remember sorrow
sad eyes waiting

you will leave me you will
leave me like a rosary
you rubbed

the small blister of truth
the sore you picked red
never wanting it to heal

July, 1949

in the end, there is only the sadness
the stale smoke from other cigarettes
the paper-wrapped glass that's not clean

in my dreams, there are always tiles falling
dark hairs in the sink
yellow stains on the back of the soap

this string of motels like old teeth
rotting under red lips, putrid
fluorescent with death

Writing the Writer: Dear Cue

I love the sleek shine of your forehead
rubbed too smooth for hair
the hard right cheek with the crease
that smiles like a gun

I love the gilt cracks in your teeth
the dry skin, the small lines on your lips
the way your throat turns to the light

your voice smooth as worn marble
your tongue cool as the grave
and your burnt sugar sweetness
pushing down

part two: 1949

Writing the Writer: Dear Cue

these are the late days of tennis
private lessons in sunlight and shade
secret smiles and white linen, gut cords
strung too tight for the game

these are the hot afternoons
melting into peach twilights
pale sugared drinks damp as sweat
sticking like the seat of your car
to my thighs, the thick taste of magnolia
on our tongues

the touch and the taste and the moon
hanging heavy and sweet, suspended
tossed for the serve

Words Not Spoken: Dear Cue

the first touch to my skin
was your hand to my cheek
eyes lowered, lips to the flame

and after the first touch, the silence
pulling in on itself, the cigarette shared
between strangers

we sit side by side without speaking
your breath delicate and precise as the smoke
hanging on air

the first time I dreamed I was dreaming

the weight of your tongue in my mouth
your teeth on my lips and my eyes
closed for the kiss

and then waking
feeling only your prick in my palm
warming like stone to the touch

the kiss and the weight and the smoke
rubbed into our skin
and your tongue

the first time I
dreamed I was dreaming
and woke to your touch

with snooker it is all in the breaks

and the eye, the nerve to win
and the patience to lose
without seeming to care

and with luck

it is simply

a game, hitting
balls against balls
the more balls, the
higher the score

Breakfast

I've been dreaming this dream all my life
waiting for the smooth curve of your cheek
to fit the palm of my hand   the tight smile
as you butter burned toast

you change between meetings, forget
I am always the same

you are the shaper of dreams
the man who has archives
where others have letters
memoirs, where others have lives

I bring only myself, and the small
impossible gift you refuse to call love

this is the scene you have chosen:
tea and toast, and a straight shot of vodka
a terrible ordinary awkwardness
stiffening our bodies like starch

we curl on the couch
and look down
your words heavy
between us, pages
damp on my lap

look, you say
look

Parlour Tricks

You push pins through my flesh at a party
pressing silver through skin

everyone knows

with tricks,
the pleasure is all in the audience
all in the stillness and the pain
no one mentions

and after, like love
you feel only disgust
and the first cool draught
from a door that will always
swing open

you use the word love like your cock
to push straight to my heart
and then stop

you have done this before

for you there is only the sex
and then nothing

only your pleasure

thin and sharp as a Japanese cock
inked in on rice paper
poised and delicate
inviting the smudge

when you dream, you dream a girl bending
pouring water from a classical vase
you feel the heat of your hand
warming marble worn smooth
and the weight of the water
draws you down

all you desire is the curve of the back
the turn of the hips
and her burden

tonight you will tell me you love me
as you ask me to watch as you watch

tonight you lean down when I cry
see yourself in the mirror
tell me you want to push your
fingers to the back of my mouth
your fist through my heart

and yes
tonight is the night you almost
close your eyes when we kiss
almost promise to stay
almost stay

tonight is the night
you pretend I'm a boy
and press down

I put my arms to your neck
lips to dry lips
you push down
leaving only the sex of you
warm on my mouth
your fingerbones
stroking my hair

you hit the white clean
as the tap of your finger
ball kissing ball and the pockets
shimmer with delight

it's never a question of winning
it's playing the game
cool and precise, as the heat
from a lover's first bite

you lean over the table in silence
thighs smooth against walnut
holding your cue as tenderly
as a cigarette after love

and in this one perfect moment, there is only
the quiet tension of flesh and the sigh
as balls curve to your touch
and then fall

the small hidden ache of remembrance
drawing blood from the bone

you want to write plays
about a young girl who cries
by a door with her head to the light
you rehearse the smooth curve of her neck
the dry shake of thin limbs   the cool
shimmer of despair as she turns

you long for this dream-child, forgetting
the stale smell of her fear

you want a lover you can love without sex
who cries without tears   who leaves
without tasting betrayal
under the empty martini
the stubbed cigarette

you remember a woman who loved you
and a donkey a burro an ass
with the sign of the cross
down its back

you remember the cross
and the penis
the slow burn
of a mexican sun

tomorrow
you may remember the flies
and the handful of dollars
and how the woman-child weeps
with a mouth like a wound
black with sores

but tonight
you are dreaming a woman, a harness
a cross and a dusty grey donkey
and how your friends laughed, her ribs
cracking under the weight

some dreams are not dreams
some words remain spoken

I turn my back, hear my own undressing
and you indifferent to the click
the rub, the smooth brush of fabric
on fabric, quickly pushed down

I feel old under your fingers
my hips too wide and my skin
the pale yellow of flypaper
sticky with heat

and after, when you turn
to brush my cheek, I turn away
suddenly afraid of this
small moment of approval

and yes, I agree
this is not seductive
this stripping naked
under the cool eyes of a man
who sees two arms two legs
two eyelids pressed down
two elbows bent over breasts
pale skin green in the light

this is not erotic
and you are obscene
as you sit, fully clothed
saying no

for you there is only
the pushing down of a head
or a hand on your cock

the caress as you pull the hair back
from a face for the view

you have no time for words
and no memory   a girl is a girl
is a girl

I want to slap you   to force you
to listen   I want to say: No

My name is Dolores
write that *love*

today you will tell me again
how ugly I am, your eyes
staring over my head
your flesh slapping time

today you will lean over my bed
to the carpet below, feeling
for the packet of matches
you know won't be there

you will leave without speaking
and then stand at the door
lighting your smoke with one motion
caressing the air

this is your week for not speaking
your mouth puckered tight and your eyes
too bright to hide

this is my week to feel shame
to hear laughter
behind your locked door
the week everyone pleases
but me

this is the night when you stand
at the top of the stair
and I stand behind   dreaming
hands at the small of your back
pushing down

45

eggshell man
your high forehead
aches to be broken

your arms, tight cords
try too hard

you're afraid
your thin shoulders
will crack with the weight
of this love

little man
you are right:

your slim hands and legs
will know only the wall
and the small sudden push
from behind

I want to shake you
to tell you there is more to love
than rice paper gymnastics
more to a mouth
than the raw edge of a hole

I want to teach you that love
comes from fingers not fists
not legs in improbable places
not eyes painted dead

and if I can't show you
the sting of an ivory-carved dildo
the hate in a prick without love
I will do as you ask: paint my lips red
draw on my eyes like black stars

leave you stiff and hard
as the head of a corpse

and then, my love
we will talk

part three: 1952

you empty your tip
on the table before me
and smile

your neck heavy with grease
lashes dark as used oil, watching
the slick coinage of love
slide away

I am writing this poem to two eyes and a mouth
a turned head
I remember from dreams

eyes dark as a pool
flecked with leaves
face open as sunlight

writing the soft crease
down the cheek of a face
I could love   turning
dreams into words
to be spoken

I roll your name under my tongue
like a child with a sweet
feel the weight of my tongue
pressed to teeth

I am drunk with the forms of politeness:

dear Mister, dear
Richard, Love, Lo
and it's only a letter!

a handshake, fingers to palm
or the brush of a public farewell
your eyes close for the kiss

I hold my thumb in the palm of my hand
dream it's yours

and like a child with a sweet
the world shines, sticky and bright
with the secret

this burning, this sweetness
seems too much to bear

this pushing into my own soul with yours
the pain where we touch
the cool friction of parts
into parts

does it hurt does it slowly
then slower, then the small
moment of knowing our pain
isn't the point

photograph

there is a boy leaning
down from a chair
like a pale christmas cherub
skin fluorescent in the shadow of plants

everything around him seems golden

I want to show you
the carved groove of his back
the muscle cradling his hips
the legs falling clean from his thighs

everything about him smells sweet

I once saw this man in my window
bending over my plants in the nude
with his back to my camera

the air that he breathes
tastes of lemons

the water drips muddy and dark
and the holes in the pot bleed white roots
and the man

with the boy's voice
and thin shoulders
stands naked and laughs

this body is built for betrayal

these hips swell with deceit
holding blood like stained hands
at a fountain, cupped for the flow

pregnant is a word meaning
things that aren't said
to be full of ideas, to contain

pregnant
is the pause before silence

there are no safe steps to be taken
this small blooded seed of our loving
burrows deeper, determined to grow

I Wear White at the Wedding, you Wear Black

we say vows before three plastic ducks
in flight on a rose-printed wall

no mothers, no friends, no
maiden aunts weeping
we bring only ourselves
and the money

my wedding ring, circle of sorrow
second-hand gold for the bride

we lie as easily in sleep
as hands cupped to a palm
a child's puzzle curved
back to back   baby
curving within

and every morning the same
small turn of a head, the smile
the moving from absolute strangeness
to grace

the terrible beauty of a man
clean-limbed without clothes

learning monogamy

with the first there was only the boredom
the dull ache in a jaw held too tight
the endless burble of unwanted love

the next liked to watch
with a drink before dinner
campari and a smoke between friends

but now this sometimes plain boy
turns too still when men stare
turns away when men's hands
slip too low   I see my love
turning

and myself, surprised
stepping back from the dance

a lover, a mother, a wife
a respectable lady
five years late
I learn to speak
"no."

Flag Day

you are walking away with the veterans
no women invited or allowed

memorial days are for men

I watch you retreat across sunlight
small shoulders squared to the task

this and this, old men point
look at that

and you nod, standing in shadow
your hand to your eyes

a man-child turned solemn
by the remembrance of war

a small boy grown old
with the burden

you will be rich, very rich says the gypsy

you are the one I have always loved
in Egypt, in Greece, on the moon
I was always a princess

a princess with bracelets of flesh
and a hand lined with passion
the smooth scars of a belly pulled tight
my adornments of love

we will be rich, very rich
in the next life but one
we will always be lovers

sometimes this child I call monster
holds my heart in its hands
eight fingers, two thumbs
squeezing hard

sometimes I feel baby floating
like a salt water minnow
nose bumping the bowl
feasting on dark bubbles
in a cushion of blood

sometimes it's an eel
the greased colour of cream
slipping sideways through
water to shore

this fleshy pale slug of our loving
digging deeper to feed on the root

this is the lady of the house fixing meals
this is her waxing her floors
this is the woman of the household
cleaning toilets, washing windows
ordering three pints of cream
and the paper on credit

this is the little treasure
baking anything she likes
fixing meals three times a day
licking spoons, clipping coupons
reading slick magazines

this is the better half greeting my husband
in a thin cotton frock and with something
I once heard called a martini
although we call it gin

or at home with a bathrobe and curlers
a book and a bottle of beer

this is the wife of the man of the house
doing dishes, folding clothes
using Ivory and Ajax and Mr Clean
this is the girl who married the boy
who's almost a father who is happy

these are the photos
of home renovations: Richard

fixing the tap
Richard

painting the bedroom
laying linoleum, badly

Richard out of focus
back to camera

the album no one will want
when we die, the images

we will use when we are old
to explain

the small breaks in the dreams
we call life

I watch onions left too long in the larder
spread pale fingers of shoots
potatoes wrinkle and fade

parents devoured by growth
until nothing remains

this is the way we have chosen:
a baby, a wedding, a life

this is the way we will count
down the days: short sharp kicks
as you ask me to smile
the small bones of my face
smudged away

this is the way it is ending
dirty laundry, no money, a dog,
a baby already a monster
already dying

this is the way I have chosen
the man of my dreams

photograph, summer

I see my love smiling
into the camera

leaning on a brightly waxed car
arms folded, legs crossed
dungarees faded and stained

standing like a child
with a favourite toy
shirt pushed high on the elbows
dark hair catching the light

looking-glass still
shining on

this small perfect moment
should not have happened:

no one told you not to smile
not to squint hard and stand
thin arms folded and tanned

laughing
looking into the sun

lately we've been dreaming Alaska
pink shadows, blue drifts
sunset streets the colour of gold
and a winter of moonlight

air catches the back of your throat
crisp and cool, clean as the first
taste of water

and waterfalls, frozen in motion
leave their colours behind

I want to write poems to the back of your neck
take your soft dark hairs in my hands
and shine them with love

I want to hold your throat like a bird
and feel your bones beat
put my heart on your heart
and stay silent

I want to dream giving you children
you don't know you want
feel flesh grow with the weight of our love
floating through crowds
like a streetcar

I want
you only you   only you
and to know   this dark silent singing
will be heard

For the benefit of old-fashioned readers who wish to follow the destinies of the "real people" beyond the "true" story . . . . Mrs. "Richard F. Schiller" died in childbed, giving birth to a stillborn girl, on Christmas day 1952 . . . . no ghosts walk.

John Ray, Jr., Ph.D.
Foreword, *Lolita*

Kim Morrissey

Kim Morrissey's *Batoche* (Coteau Books, 1989; reprinted 1990 and 1992) won the 1987 Saskatchewan Writers Guild Contest judged by Gwendolyn MacEwen and D.G. Jones, won third prize in the 1987 CBC National Literary Awards, was short-listed for the 1990 Gerald Lampert Memorial Award (Best First Book of Poetry, League of Canadian Poets), is being taught in universities in Canada, Britain and Germany, and is now in its third printing.

Her critically acclaimed satiric re-examination of Freud, *Dora: A Case of Hysteria*, was produced by Steven Gregg at Wheatland Theatre in Regina, Saskatchewan in 1987 and in Louisville, Kentucky in 1990. *Dora* was first produced by BBC Radio 3 in 1991.